The

History of

Eyelash Extensions

and Other Eye Treatments

LUXURY PRODUCTS AT COMPETITIVE PRICES. FEATURING OUR RED RUBY VOLUME ADHESIVE

QUALITY, IN-DEPTH TRAINING LOCATED IN LOS ANGELES. WE ALSO TRAVEL THE US BRINGING OUR CLASSIC AND VOLUME TRAINING TO YOU

SINFUL LASHES

since 2001

LUXURY PRODUCTS & QUALITY TRAINING

1-818-970-7151
sinfullashes@gmail.com
www.sinfullashes.com

The History of Eyelash Extensions and Other Eye Treatments
Copyright © 2014 Louise Prunty

The following information was gathered from public domain sources, the publisher is mot responsible for any errors or omissions in this book.

Chrysalis House Publishing
Louise Prunty
Lower Ground
7 Newton Place
Glasgow
G3 7PR
United Kingdom

publishinguk@me.com
www.chrysalishousepublishing.com

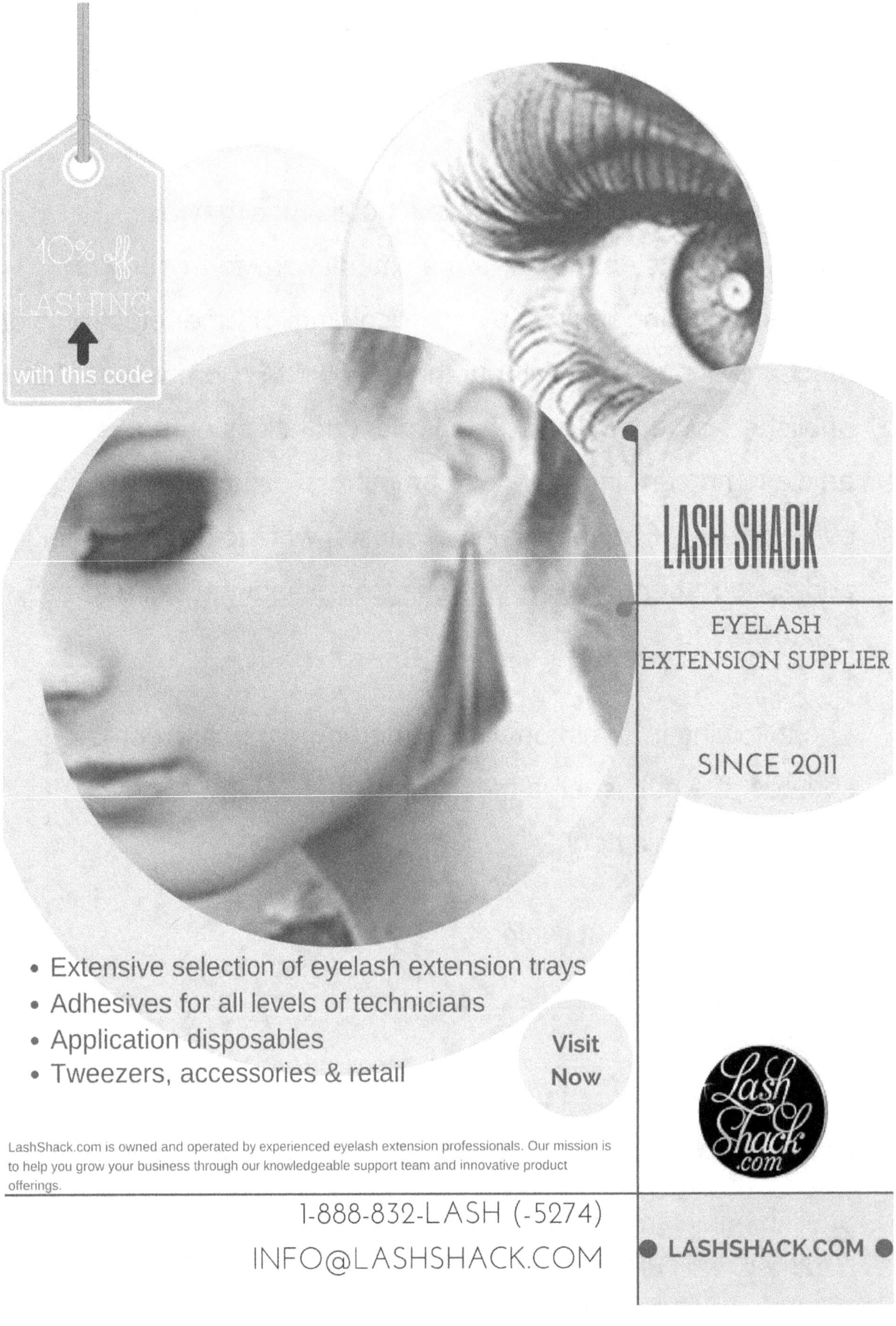

10% off
LASHINC
with this code
LASH SHACK
EYELASH
EXTENSION SUPPLIER
SINCE 2011
• Extensive selection of eyelash extension trays
• Adhesives for all levels of technicians
• Application disposables
• Tweezers, accessories & retail
Visit Now
Lash Shack .com
LashShack.com is owned and operated by experienced eyelash extension professionals. Our mission is to help you grow your business through our knowledgeable support team and innovative product offerings.
1-888-832-LASH (-5274)
INFO@LASHSHACK.COM
LASHSHACK.COM

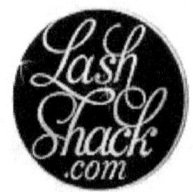

The History of Eyelash Extensions

Introduction

Eyelash extensions are the fastest growing beauty treatment in the world. Originally introduced in the early 1900s, over the past century the process of enhancing the length of one's eyelashes has become a fundamental element of cosmetics.

Nowadays eyelash enhancing is among the most profitable sectors in the beauty industry, spurred on by Hollywood fashion and advancements in technology that have made materials and adhesives safer to adorn than ever before.

In modern times the attachment process is a profession, and has gained the support of governing bodies, such as BABTAC, The Guild of Professional Beauty Therapists, Lash Inc, ABT and NEESA to name a few. 'Lash Technicians', 'Lash Artists', and 'Lash Stylists' are now highly employable occupations; but the world of cosmetics wasn't always this way...

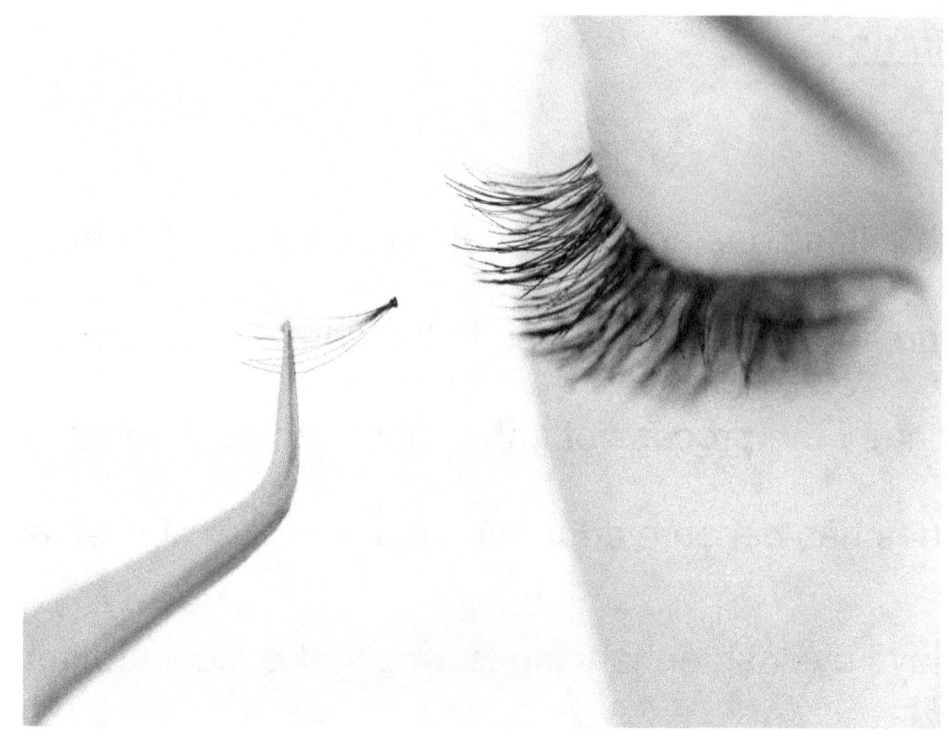

Who invented eyelash extensions?

Famed filmmaker D.W. Griffith is often credited as the creator of eyelash extensions. During the making of his 1916 movie *Intolerance*, he felt that something was missing while studying the costume of actress Seena Owen. He decided that the problem was her eyes.

"They should be twice as large and look supernatural."

– D.W. Griffith

He ordered his wigmaker to glue a pair of lashes to Owen's eyelids using spirit gum. While he managed to achieve the "baby doll" look he desired, Owen suffered from very severe eye problems throughout the following days. Luckily for Griffith, her scenes were already wrapped.

But, Hollywood legend aside, Griffith certainly wasn't the original creator of eyelash extensions. In fact, five years prior in 1911 a Canadian woman named Anna Taylor patented the first artificial eyelash in the U.S. Additionally, in 1915 German born Charles Nestle (aka Karl Nessler) manufactured false eyelashes and even owned his own hair salon in New York which specialized in lash treatments.

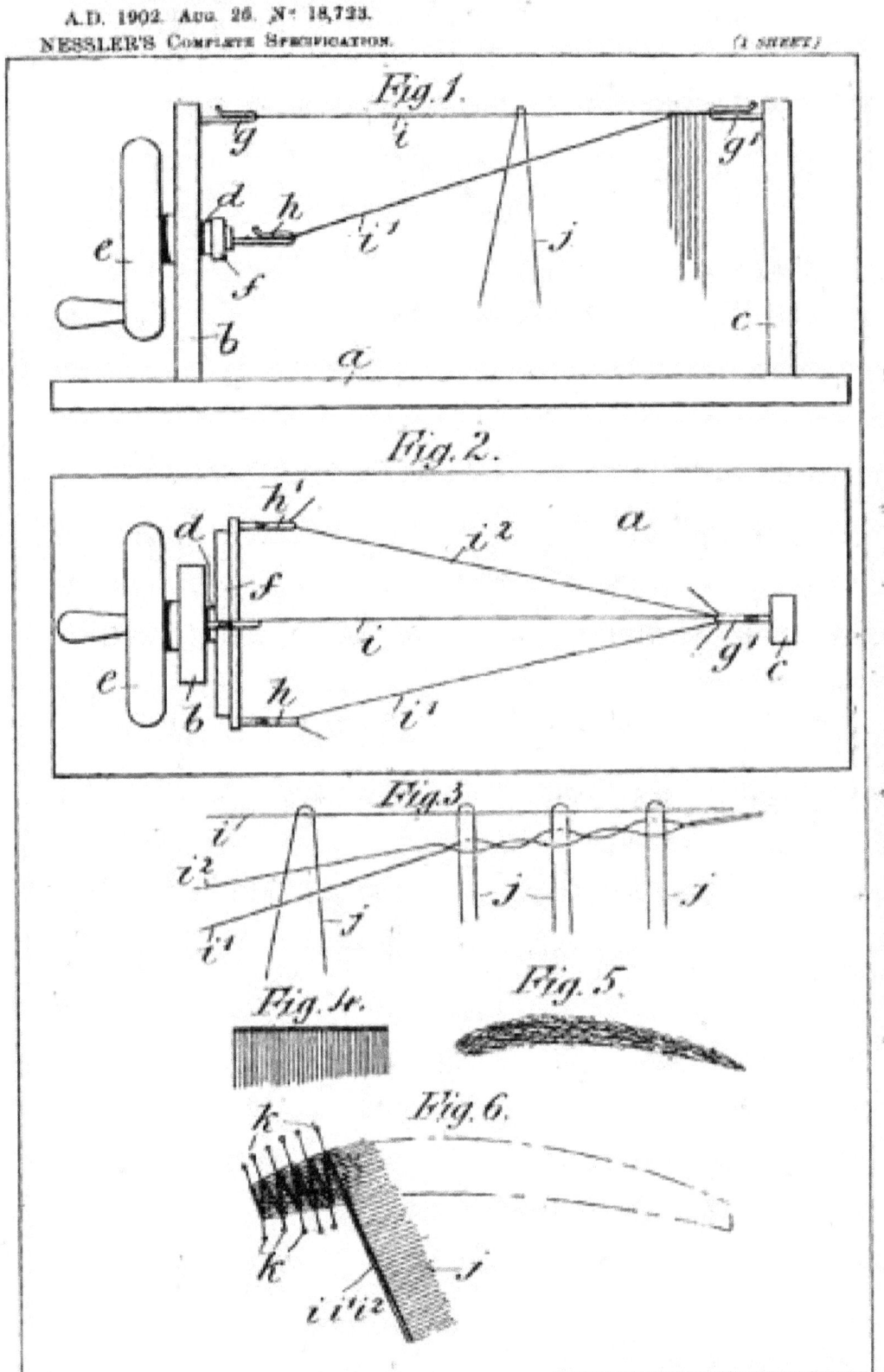

However, the true route of eyelash extensions can be traced back much, much further.

One of the earliest known attempts to enhance eyelashes was during the time of the Ancient Egyptians, when royalty used a black powder called kohl to protect their eyes against sand, dust and bugs. However, this was to provide practical benefits, rather than cosmetic.

Ancient Eyelash Treatments

They say that the eyes are the window to the soul, so it's hardly surprising that they pose a significant impact on history. Since the dawn of modern civilization people have strived to make their eyes and lashes more beautiful. Archaeological digs dating back as far as the Mesopotamia and Assyria era even show evidence of precious stones being ground and used to decorate the faces of women. But the earliest known evidence of eye cosmetics dates back 4,000 years.

Mascara was developed far before Maybelline invented the name in the 20th century. Faced with the difficult living

11

conditions of the harsh dry desert, the Egyptians sought to combat the problem by developing a solution that would protect their eyes from the elements. However, evidence suggests that while the Egyptians sought a medicinal solution to their problem, for centuries they strived to integrate medicine into cosmetics and fashion. This fashion was designed to honour their religious beliefs.

At the time kohl was the most widely used eye and eyelash treatment in the Middle East, and even today many still use it. The eyelash mascara was created using a variety of ingredients such as charcoal, soot, honey, water and crocodile stool! The result was darkened eyelashes and eyebrows that protected against sand blown in the wind, microorganisms and other types of harmful dust. But aside from the cosmetic and practical benefits, it also had religious significance. The ancient Egyptians believed that the wearer's soul was protected against harmful spirits. Therefore, the application was often part of a bigger ritualistic procedure.

There is a great deal of evidence to suggest that eye treatments were also a luxury cosmetic feature of this time. The pharaohs were buried with luxuries of life and cosmetics are almost always found hidden inside the tombs. King Tut's tomb, for example, was opened in 1922 and archaeologists found cosmetics that dated back to 10,000 BC. These eye cosmetics were not only old, but still perfectly usable.

Other early evidence of eye cosmetics was found in the ruins of Babylon, such as tweezers and brow brushes, suggesting that eyelashes and eyebrow treatments were common practice. During this time it is thought that both men and women wore eye shadow, eyeliner and various other eyelash and eyebrow enhancers.

The Egyptian Influence

The influence of Egyptian cosmetic and chemical eye treatments cannot be understated. Their products spread further than the confines of their country, eventually finding a home in Greece and Rome; whose cultures welcomed them into their fashion. In ancient Greece, however, the more natural look was preferred. This changed during the 4th century BC, when Grecian women started using false eyelashes and eyebrows made from ox hair.

During the fall of Rome the entire cosmetic industry in Europe declined. Eye treatments were considered vanity items adorned only by the rich and powerful. This didn't change until the reign of Queen Victoria – hundreds of years later – between 1837 and 1901. It was during this time that cosmetic products and fashion became an integral aspect of living the mid/high class lifestyle.

The illusion of dark and longer eyelashes soon became an obsession for many post-Edwardian women; and due to the significant rise in public promotion, they often spent hours each day applying makeup to their faces... and then came Hollywood.

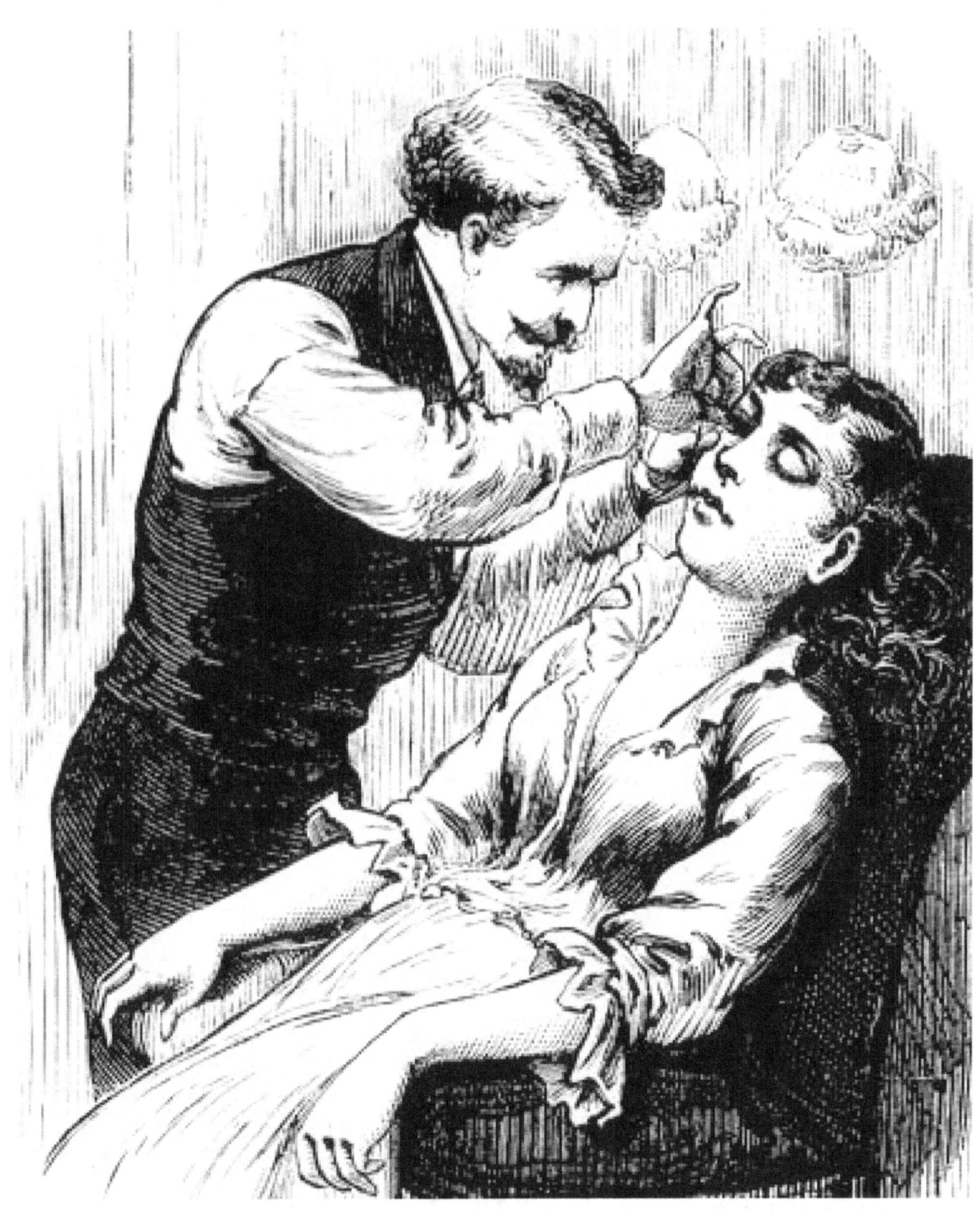

1882 Fringed eyelashes being sewed on to brighten eyes

(from McLaughlin, 1972).

After D.W. Griffith

Whether or not D.W. Griffith should be credited as the 'inventor' of modern false eyelashes is debatable due to Anna Taylor and Charles Nestle; however, his influence on the industry cannot be understated as he certainly popularised their use. After *Intolerance*, Seena Owen's false eyelashes were soon adapted into other Hollywood movies. These lashes were created using human hair that was hand woven with fine gauze. Over the coming years popularity in false eyelashes continued to soar.

In 1917 Maybelline was born, and soon after, became a market leader in eye cosmetics – though namely "eyelash darkener", which they started to call "mascara" in 1933. It was around this time that they started producing their first commercially available false eyelashes which, by the mid-1930s, women were enjoying all over the world.

There were significant breakthroughs in the eyelash extension scene during the 40s and 50s. Cutting edge designs and new application methods were being developed by virtually all of the major cosmetic brands. In addition, they were becoming more and more natural looking than ever before.

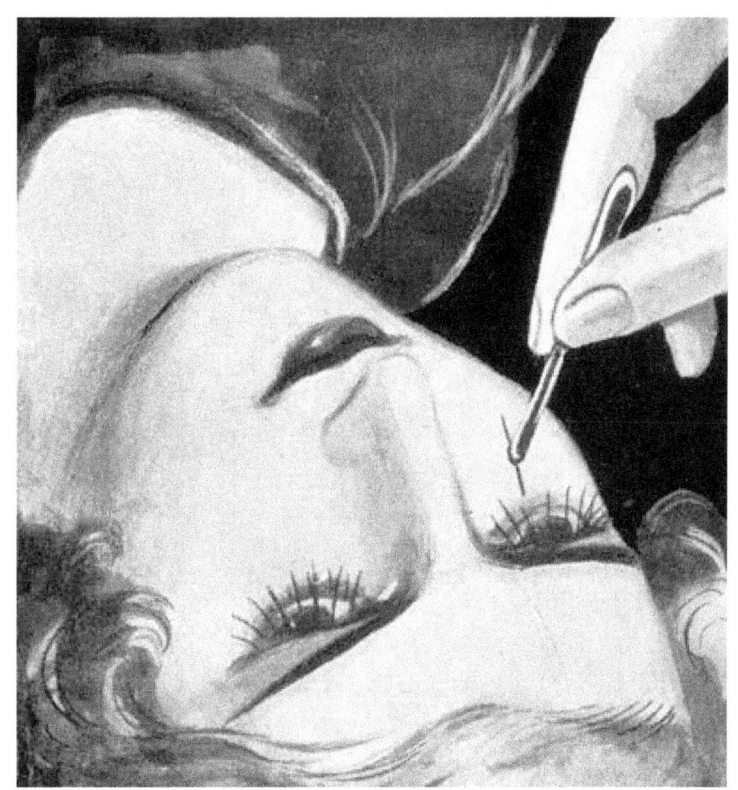

Growing Popularity

When English model, actress and singer Twiggy became the 'it girl' in Hollywood, people were fascinated with her doe-eyed lashes. Cosmetic companies started to place more emphasis on expanding their ranges in order to capitalize on her popularity. Lashes were in all the fashion magazines, and subsequently, they were asked for by women in virtually every beauty parlour in the United States; and it didn't matter how fake they looked – the bolder the better.

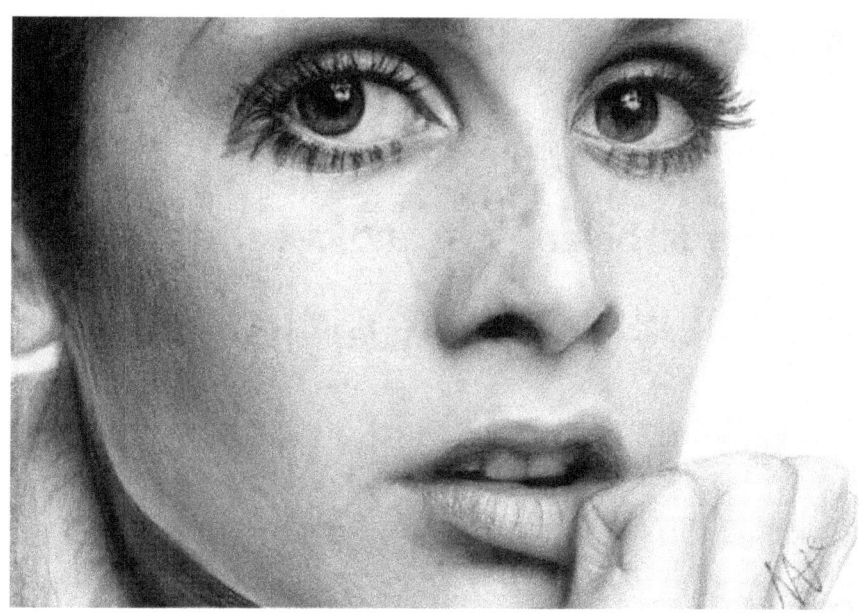

Image Credit: <u>*Aberdeen Journal*</u>

Modern Times

Fast forward to the present and eyelashes are a standard feature of cosmetics and day-to-day life. Driven by sex appeal and celebrity trends, they are now one of the most popular items in cosmetics. Artists such as Nicole Kidman, Gwen Stefani and Naomi Campbell all wear eyelash extensions and have inspired women all over the world to incorporate them into their look.

How Have Eyelash Extensions Progressed?

Since false eyelashes were first invented the whole industry has advanced on a decade-by-decade basis. Nowadays governing bodies implement safety precautions; new products must be deemed 'fit' before use; and beauty therapists must train in the art before they're considered qualified to undertake the task. In Europe there has been a recent shake up in cosmetic legislation which requires specific labelling, safety testing, stability testing of cosmetic products including 'at home' eyelash extensions and professional eyelash extension products such as adhesive and de-bonder.

The Advancement of Governing Bodies

During the early 1900s there were no official accreditation procedures. Wigmakers, hairdressers or anyone within the cosmetic industry was deemed qualified to create and apply eyelash extensions. Due to the lack of safety precautions women often encountered eye-health problems, such as the case with Seena Owen.

One of the biggest changes to the industry over the past 100 years was the formation of professional governing bodies. HABIA is the government appointed body for looking after hair and beauty standards in the UK. The Guild of Beauty Therapists is a business established in the UK but is one of the more popular accrediting companies. This organization contains over 8,000 members throughout the country (2014); many of which specialize solely in eyelash extensions.

There are also many other companies which 'accredit' eyelash technicians or eyelash training courses. I believe it is only a matter of time before the UK government will introduce mandatory registration with a sole organisation, at this point some organisations may merge others might be out of business.

In the USA you need to be state registered to apply eyelash extensions. There are also professional associations beginning to service the market.

Types of Eyelash Extensions

When false eyelashes were first commercially available the only variation was the length. It took decades until the industry started to stray away from real hair and dabble with other materials and styles. Nowadays there are lashes to suit virtually any occasion or look.

Natural Lashes

Natural lashes have a more fragile appearance. While they boost extra length and thickness, they don't look false at a glance. These lashes are often used during daytime outings when a more discreet look is desired.

Full Lashes

Full lashes became popular in the early 2000s, and are much thicker than natural lashes and generally considered too much for everyday wear. They are great for photos and, therefore, regularly used by models and actors. In fact, the further away the subject the more prominence they have. Full lashes are usually all blunt and the same length.

Long and Short Lashes

The beauty about long and short lashes is that no two extensions will be the same. These lashes are varying lengths and may even contain criss-crossing. They are perfect for dates or when a more dramatic look is sought.

Individual Lashes

Many women find individual lashes tedious as they must be attached one-by-one; however, they can look far more natural than strip eyelashes where the eyelid meets the lashline. Application is professionally done by a qualified eyelash technician and typically takes between one and three hours depending on the look required. Once applied, most people will require an infill (touch up) at every 2 -3 weeks. Individual attachments were performed by geishas in Japan long before extensions were commercially available.

Cluster Lashes

Cluster lashes are clumps of lashes that have been bound together to form a "v" shape. They come in many densities and can be created using a wide array of materials. Application time is shorter than individual lashes and typically takes between 20 and 30 minutes. They can last 2 - 3 days.

Strip Lashes

Strip lashes are without a doubt the easiest lashes to adhere, making them suitable for one-day events such as runway shows. Strip lashes will typically take a few minutes to attach and will last all day and night; however, with the emergence of new and better quality adhesives, people are tempted to leave them on for days! I really hate the idea of this personally as I'm obsessed by keeping clean eyelashes, but also the weight of strip lashes can be too heavy and prolonged wear can be damaging.

Knotted Lash Extensions

Knotted eyelash extensions were first created in Japan in the 1960s. They are synthetic and will have a small knot at the tip of the cluster in order to create a larger surface area for the adhesive. While this can make them longer lasting and easier to attach, they are noticeable and will look false. In addition, people often complain that the knots make the eyes feel heavier.

Knot Free Lash Extensions

Knot free lash extensions do not contain a cluster of lashes at the base; therefore, they look lighter and more real. While this can make them more difficult to apply, people rarely complain about comfort.

Many years ago most people couldn't tell the difference between lash construction and application methods; however, to the wearer the variance couldn't be more noticeable. Not just from a visual perspective, but also from a practical point of view. However in recent years people are much more educated on the different types of eye treatments and lash extensions available and can tell if someone is wearing strips, clusters or individual eyelash extensions.

Eyelash Extension Materials

False eyelashes are usually created using synthetic hair, however you can also get fox hair, human hair, mink hair or Siberian mink hair; materials can vary depending on the manufacturer. Contrary to popular belief the most expensive designs aren't always the most realistic. Sometimes it's a more doe-eyed, fantastical look that's required, which could be associated to a material of less 'quality'.

The quality of eyelash extensions is one of the most important things a professional eyelash technician requires from their supplier and clients are becoming increasingly aware of the differences in quality.

Synthetic

Synthetic lashes were first introduced to the industry in 1975. They are generally the most rugged material and are created using a grade-A fibre that can be curved to replicate the natural shape of an eyelash. Synthetic lashes are usually more glossy in appearance than other materials; however, they're not as natural looking. Due to their shiny and denser appearance they are often favoured by the younger generation.

Mink

Mink lashes first became commercially available in Japan in 1967. They are commonly manufactured using other materials in order to give them the same properties – softness, flexibility, appearance, etc. – as human hair. They are long lasting and will not curl if wet. Mink lashes are often favoured by those who have brittle lashes as they are light and rarely fall off.

Siberian Mink

Siberian Mink lashes are ultra light and soft – making them highly flexible – and are considered to be the most luxurious on the market. Lash and curl length will vary, which makes them look very natural. In addition, they will often change shape when in contact with water. Like standard mink lashes they are light and will rarely fall off – even when pressure is applied – making them a favourite among those with brittle lashes.

Fox Hair

Fox hair is one of the most expensive eyelash materials as it's very light and looks natural without mascara. While they are generally above the price range for the average user, they're commonly sought after by the rich and famous and can often been seen on the red carpet. For this reason they have significantly risen in popularity since the early 2000s.

Human Hair

The original false eyelashes were made from human hair. They are more expensive than synthetic lashes and the differences are usually very clear as they look natural and light. However, people will often choose synthetic due to the broader range of choice.

Since eyelash extensions found their way into the mainstream, so have the headings, "100% human made", and "100% human hair quality". While lashes adorning these titles may seem like a good deal, they will rarely withstand the test of time. In fact, these types of eyelashes are often made for mannequins. Human lashes are generally recommended for people seeking comfort, quality, softness and reliability.

Eyelashes for Eye Shapes

Back in the early 20th century there was only one type of false eyelash, nowadays there are ranges to suit everyone; from the colour of their hair to the shape of their eyelids. Everybody's eye shape is different; therefore, the individual effect of the lash can significantly vary from one to another. Below is a list of different types of lashes and how they can compliment varying looks.

Round Eyes

Those with big round eyes regularly wear long thin lashes that fan upwards. This makes the eyes look larger and accentuates the circular shape.

Almond Eyes

Any form of eyelash seems to compliment almond shaped eyes; however, many celebrities with this shape – Taylor Swift, Cheryl Cole – will often accentuate the outer corners for a cat-like similarity that fans outwards. This style became very popular in 2010.

Hooded Eyes

Ladies with hooded eyes often wear lashes that have strands of various lengths, with the longest directly above the pupil. Many also place lashes on the lower outer corner for a more wide-eyed look.

Mono Lid

Most women with a mono lid (no crease) will use fanned out false eyelashes. In recent years model Liu Wen has popularized this look.

Some lash extensions are specifically designed for certain eye shapes. Most beauty therapists will be able to recommend a specific design or material to ensure the extension compliments the look and isn't out of place.

Eyelash Extension Adhesives

The type of eyelash glue that's used can make a huge difference to the look and feel. The first false eyelashes were glued to the eyelid using spirit gum. This, however, proved to be irritable. Over the years various other adhesives were invented by cosmetic brands to match the colour of specific skin tones.

Strip Lash Adhesive

Strip lashes tend to be the most popular; however, they're generally not very strong. In most circumstances it will last for about 24 hours. Nowadays most adhesives are latex-free and available in clear/white or black/dark. Strip lashes rarely require lash remover as they usually come off with a gentle tug.

Individual Lash Adhesive

Individual lash adhesive is usually stronger than strip lash adhesive. In addition, the smell can also be quite overpowering. Lash remover must be used when removing individual lashes as there is a danger of pulling out natural lashes.

Surgical Lash Adhesive

Surgical lash adhesive is rarely stocked by cosmetic stores because unless it's properly applied it can be highly dangerous. Only qualified cosmetologists, beauticians, makeup artists and lash specialists trained to use this adhesive should use it.

Selecting the eyelash adhesive / glue is almost as important as selecting the lash itself. Without an adhesive that matches the colour of the surrounding skin, or contains a strong bonding, the lashes will look out of place and suffer from fast degradation.

For semi permanent eyelash extensions cyanoacrylate based adhesive is used, this forms a strong bond between the natural lash and the lash extension.

Adhesive types are developing rapidly. In 2008 a flexible glue was developed by Caledonian Therapy Academy, this was brought to market through research done by Louise Prunty (then a director of the company) on adhesives in other industries.

The concept of a flexible adhesive for the eyelash industry was born from cosmetic development on existing adhesives in the electronics industry.

Using a flexible adhesive meant the lashes bent with the adhesive and a sealant was not required.

Between 2012 - 2014 many new adhesives have entered the market place some slower set and others fast set, there is also everything in between to cater for beginners, intermediate and advanced lash technicians.

The Development of Eyelash Extension Education

Since the 1990s various educational establishments have been developing eyelash extension courses which provide professional accreditation. Many of these courses are not only designed to teach students how to apply false lashes, but to also help improve safety within the industry and develop new products.

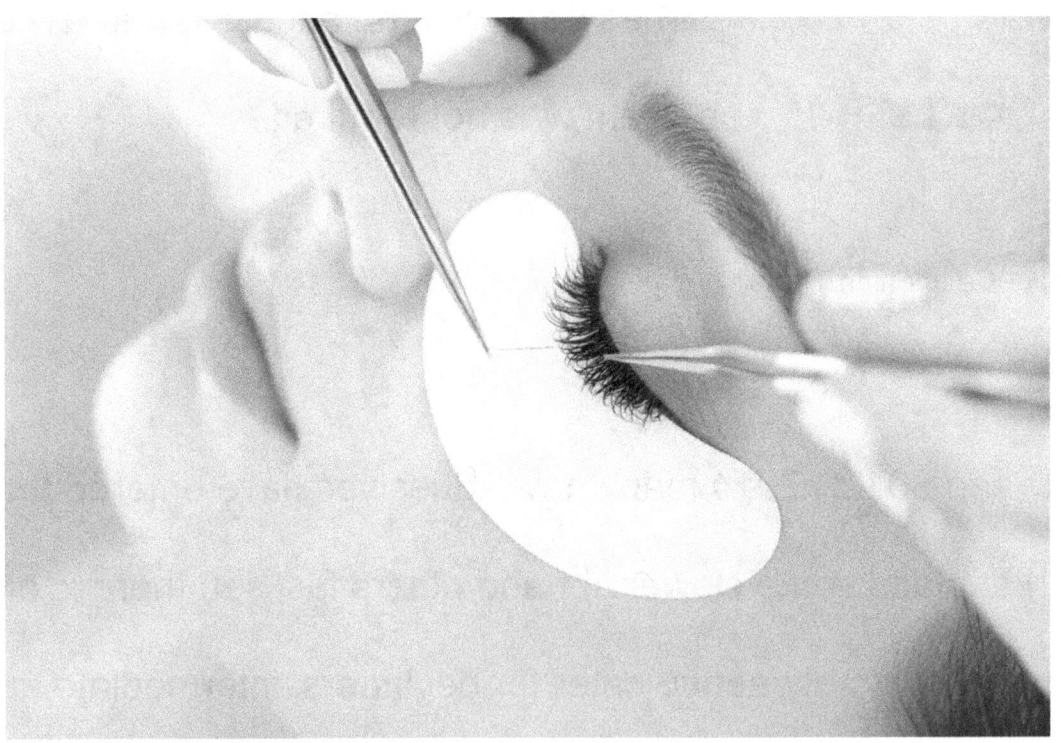

Most courses are short-term, lasting from a few days to a few weeks, and require practical exercises practiced on a volunteer model. Students usually receive an official accreditation when they deliver a minimum of two case studies and demonstrate safe application under inspection.

Organisations that provide these accreditation include:

- The British Association of Beauty Therapy and Cosmetology

- The Guild of Beauty Therapists

- Lash Inc

- Professional Beauty Direct

- Associated Beauty Therapists

Having a qualification under one of these industry bodies is usually a pre-requisite in order to find employment in the cosmetics industry. After acquiring industry accreditation experts estimate that beauty therapists could earn approximately £25,000 per year (as of 2014) with just one eyelash application per day.

Application Procedures

Semi permanent eyelash extensions are not to be confused with typical eyelash extensions, which are made with strips or lashes knotted together and applied with a specialist adhesive. With semi permanent eyelash extensions neither the extension lash or adhesive touches the eyelid, meaning that the extension will only fall out when the natural eyelash falls out. This results in a far more natural and lighter solution.

Semi permanent eyelash extensions are applied to one lash at a time. Celebrities regularly adorn them on red carpet events; they can be worn in swimming pools, saunas and gyms – pretty much any activity; and do not require the use of removal products at all.

Before any eyelashes are applied the natural lashes are measured to determine what length and thickness is most suitable. To actually bond the false eyelash the beauty therapist will isolate an individual lash using a pair of tweezers and then attach each lash using an invisible seal. This will instantly open up the eyes and give them a lift.

Lifespan

Providing aftercare procedures are taken into account and the individual treats their extensions with respect, there's no reason why semi-permanent eyelashes won't last as long as the natural lash. Most people will shed around two lashes per day; therefore, in-fills are generally required every two to five weeks in order to keep them looking full – this is generally recommended when around 50% of the false eyelashes are remaining.

Most beauty therapists will charge a smaller fee for in-fills; however, they may have a specific time period with which the in-fill appointment must be booked. Those who miss this appointment period will often have to pay for a full set of lashes instead as more than 50% of the natural lashes may have shed.

Preparing for Eyelash Extensions

- Individuals are encouraged not to wear any makeup prior to an appointment – especially water proof mascara.

- Eye makeup should not be removed using an oil-based makeup remover as it will affect the bonding process and make the new lashes weaker.

- Individuals should not wear water proof mascara or curl their eyelashes 48 hours prior to the appointment as it can negatively affect the bonding process.

- Eyelash tints should not be carried out 48 hours prior to the appointment as it can negatively affect the bonding process.

- Contact lenses should be removed before lash extension treatments as the eyes will be shut throughout the duration of the bonding process.

Aftercare

- Eyelash extensions should not be exposed to excessive heat such as sunbeds and steam rooms for at least 48 hours after application.

- Eyelash extensions should not get wet for at least 24 hours after application.

- Oil based mascaras should not be used while eyelash extensions are in place. Oil will dissolve the glue and cause the extensions to drop off. In addition, the oil can build up and cause eye infections.

- Eyes must not be rubbed and a soft touch is required when cleaning the lash area.

- Any oil based makeup remover should not be used. Simple non-oil based eye makeup removers are recommended.

- Liquid eyeliner and cream based eye shadow should not be used. Pencil eyeliner and powder eye shadow is okay.

Only with the correct pre and post-application procedures will semi-permanent eyelashes actually remain. Once the lashes have been attached there is not much one can't do. After the post 48 hour waiting period individuals should feel free to shower, swim, sleep and workout as if they weren't attached.

Most semi-permanent eyelash application procedures will take around two hours from beginning to end; however, this can heavily depend on the number of extensions that are to be applied.

Japan's Influence on Eyelash Technology

False eyelashes play a very important part in Japanese cosmetics. In fact, false eyelashes have been popular on a mainstream level for over 70 years – ever since renowned make up company KOJI released their tsuke-matsuge in the 1940s. To understand the history one must first understand KOJI's motivation for creating this pioneering product.

KOJI was inspired to develop their extensive range of tsuke-matsuge by the geisha. After climbing into the mainstream, changes were made to ensure each and every new design matched the needs of consumers of that particular market.

Timeline of the False Eyelash Industry in Japan

1947: Japan's first ever false eyelashes became available – tsuke-matsuge. Up until this time the geisha women would craft their own false eyelashes by hand by knitting them together, one by one, from hairs plucked from their head. While these false eyelashes were truly beautiful, it was a long and tedious process.

False eyelash brands started to develop, staring with EYELASH – adopted as the brand name for KOJI.

The lashes that were released were nicknamed BAKO "red box".

Image Credit: _KOJI_

1955: The revolutionary original design was reinvented with new packaging. This featured a PVC base instead of thin paper.

1965: No. 19 eyelashes also started using brand new coloured fibres rather than just the standard black.

1967: The increasing popularity of false eyelashes throughout the 1960s paved the way for new designs, and in 1967 the first ever mink eyelashes were created. These lashes provided a more realistic look than any other materials of the time, and closely resembled the original hand made geisha creations of the previous decades.

1970: New and more daring designs started to emerge, starting with the No. 22 eyelash, which featured different colours and materials.

1973: The first set of DUO type lashes were released. This was around the same time that the mini skirt was popularised in fashion – a look which helped spike popularity of extensions.

1975: The first Eyelash Mellow type series was born, introducing the world of synthetic fibres to the beauty industry. This made false eyelashes even stronger than natural lashes. The term "Brilliant Eyelash" was used to emphasize their significance and was party responsible for them being such a big hit in Japan.

1984: Eyelash Minette was launched, introducing Japan and the rest of the world to higher quality products.

1991: All KOJI packaging was updated on their lashes to create what they are today (2014).

1995: Throughout the following decades very little occurred. Popularity didn't increase, but didn't decrease either. In 1995, however, a brand new false eyelash was invented aimed specifically at teenage girls – Matsuge Mate. This "accent" eyelash was used to accentuate the corners of the eyes.

1999: Bead eyelashes and other, even more daring designs started to emerge. Many of these more colourful lashes were created specifically for young girls.

2006: During the early 2000s false eyelash popularity in the western world soared; however, for the first time in history Japan was trailing behind. Eventually TAKAKO was released, which were designed specifically for modern women and brought eyelashes back to the height of popularity.

2007: Speedy eyelashes were born – lashes that could be attached without adhesive. These could be applied with just one single step, which was a major innovation in eyelash technology.

Japanese eyelash manufacturers created many of the designs that the major brands use today. They were over half a century ahead of the west and continue to shock and awe the industry with new innovative designs.

Semi permanent eyelash extensions:

The invention of the technique is credited to Mr Daniel Dinh originally from Vietnam but live in the USA. He filed and was granted a patent for eyelash extensions in 2006. Mr Dinh was encouraged to file a patent from Pricilla Presley who loved his work and thought he should protect his technique. However it is known in the industry that a Mr Paing from Korea had been teaching a very similar technique for over 20 years. I do not have any other facts other that what I have read in the public domain however Mr Paing is often thought of as the creator of semi permanent eyelash extensions and Mr Dinh as the person who brought it to the US and other countries outside of Asia.

Product Development:

Eyelash extension products are in a constant stage of development. Lashes have changed at the rate of new plastics and machinery. At one time lashes were thick, looked and felt like plastic. Lashes now have the look of real lashes and feel almost like a natural lash, soft & flexible. There has also been development in de-bonder. At first there was on a liquid debonder, now there are other options in cream, gel, oil and paste.

* See Adhesives - Page 34

The Volume Technique:

Volume lashes are individual lash application using very thin, soft, light extensions.

It is very important to count how many multiple extensions you are going to apply on one natural lash, so as not to cause any stress.

Olga Dobronravova and Olga Volkova are considered the inventors of volume lashes as we know it today.

Olga Dobronravova is originally from Russia, she started to experiment with thinner lashes around the year 2009. The technique developed then was called 2D and 3D lashes using 0.15mm lashes and then 0.10mm diameter which was the thinnest available at the time.

Olga Volkova spent time leaning this technique and looked for ways to innovate from this work. Olga Volkova asked her manufacturer to produce thinner lashes 0.07mm and she came up with first volume technique for 4D-6D, which is called Hollywood volume, using finger tips to create a fan.

Volume Pickup Methods:

© Loreta Jasilionyte

Professional Profile of Loreta Jasilionyte.

Loreta Jasilionyte is the owner of Flawless L`Lashes Academy and has invented several Volume lash pick up techniques. At the moment there are 7. Why so many?

While observing students, Loreta noticed which steps can be hardest for students while they trying to create perfect "fan".

Old habits such as, the way you hold tweezers, while suitable for classic lash extensions are not always best for Volume lashes. Also different brand lashes comes with either more or less sticky part on the strip, which can make it difficult to form a nice "fan". One technique is not always suitable for everyone.

We know that there are three main Volume lash pick up methods: Fanning them on the strip, using finger tips, using tweezers. But fanning lashes on the strip does not necessarily have to be done just one way.

Loreta discovered several different techniques on how to fan lashes easier on the strip, to meet every students individual needs. At the moment Loreta offers 6 different Volume techniques, giving a choice to students to see which way works best for them.

One technique may be suitable for lashes, if they are harder to peel from the strip, other techniques can help if students have a habit of using tweezers tips, etc.

Even if you have perfect lashes, tweezers and you can create a gorgeous "fan" on the strip. It's still possible that when you peel them from the strip your fan can fall apart. Don't be quick to blame your tweezers, it could be the angle the tweezers were held that's to blame.

A 7th Volume technique is being developed and will be introduced in 2015.

The following section will include the history of other eye treatments ...

Eyelash Tinting

Eyelash Perming

Semi Permanent Mascara

The History of Eyelash Tinting

Eyelash tinting entered the market roughly a decade after eyelash extensions. In 1933 a women known only as Mrs Brown from Dayton, Ohio was encouraged by a beautician to try her new eyelash dye. She called this "revolutionary" product Lash Lure. However, the next morning Mrs Brown could not open her eyes as they were infected and riddled with ulcers. Three months later she was completely blind.

In 1934, a year after Mrs Brown's troublesome experience, another woman from Tampa, Florida applied Lash Lure to both her eyelashes and eyebrows. Within seconds her eyes started to burn, and eight days later they were covered with ulcers. When her conjunctival sac started leaking with a yellow liquid she was rushed to hospital. She died three hours later. It was established that her death occurred from septicaemia – a blood system infection – brought on by Lash Lure.

Lash Lure contained a highly toxic colouring agent called paraphenylendiamine. This substance was originally used to tint leather and clothes, and even then it was known to cause skin irritations and ulcers. The product itself contained over 30 times the accepted amount of chemical that was considered safe for human skin.

Advertisements for Lash Lure in their 1933 billboards referred to the product as a "New and improved mascara that will give you a radiating personality". At the time nobody thought that such an innocent eye cosmetic product could result in such fatal consequences.

After these horrific incidents and a number of other injuries that occurred throughout the US, eyelash dyes were completely banned in the majority

of states. This resulted in the bankruptcy of several cosmetics companies, proving that there was indeed a widespread demand for the product. Then, in 1938 the Food, Drug and Cosmetic Act was established – a bill used to regulate the advertising by introducing new labelling standards that were overseen by the FDA.

Eyelash tinting is still banned in many places. In Europe however tinting is regulated by the EU cosmetics directive and is a very popular treatment in the UK.

Image Credit: *Cosmetics and Skin*

The Evolution of Mascara

Mascara packaging is without a doubt the primary reason for the product's success. But during the Victorian era, when eye cosmetics were in heavy use, it wasn't promoted with such prominence. When Victorian style fashion ended – in approximately 1913 – a French chemist and perfumer named Eugène Rimmel created the very first non-toxic mascara. While it was messy, inconsistent and – by today's standards – extremely poor quality, it became hugely popular across Europe. In fact, it's popularity is still prevalent throughout many European countries as the name mascara is instead named Rimmel.

Image Credit: _Cosmetics and Skin_

After T. L. Williams devised a similar, yet improved form of packaging which was easier to market, his company Maybelline became the market leader in eye cosmetics. This allowed the mascara industry to break the confines of Europe and go worldwide.

Modern mascara gained significant popularity from the 1930s onwards due to the influence of Helena Rubinstain, who was one of the richest women of the 20th century. She constantly promoted the product using Hollywood as her base. In fact, throughout the 30s, 40s and 50s, it would've been uncommon to watch a woman on screen not wearing mascara.

Rubinstain's marketing vision didn't focus on one particular style. She realised that in order to really reap the rewards the industry would require widespread appeal; therefore, she made mascara a prominent feature of just about every fashion style throughout that 30 year period.

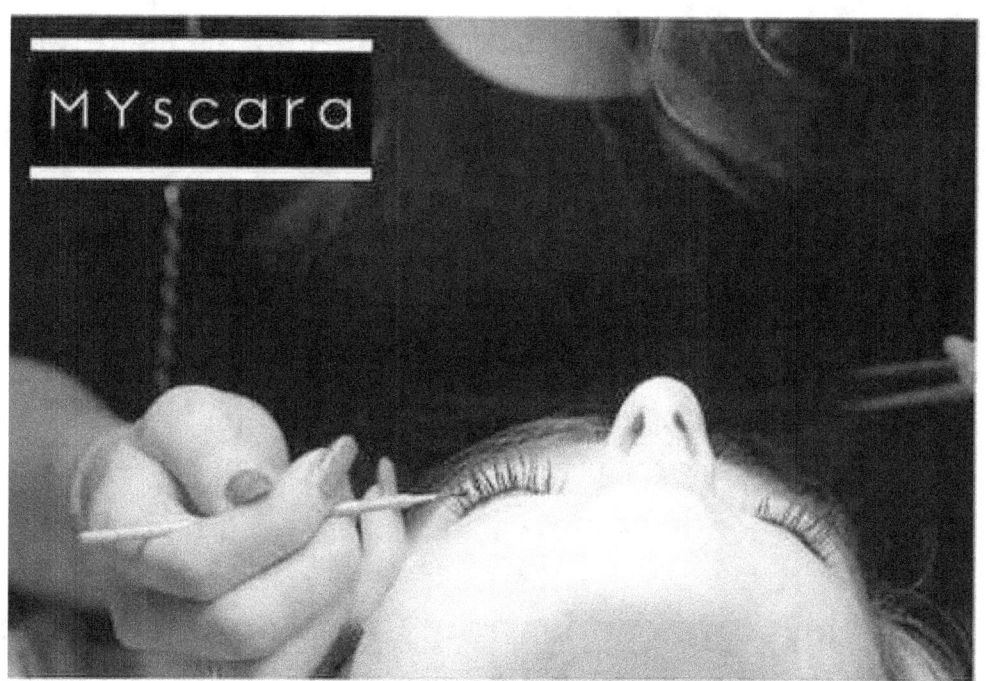

© Myscara Ireland

Semi Permanent Mascara

Semi permanent mascara was adopted in the USA in 2010,

Crybaby gained a patent for the procedure and launched the

new treatment. The treatment involved cyanoacrylate (a strong

adhesive) being mixed with a thickening fibre and painted onto

the natural lash. Lash Dip also launched their version of semi

permanent mascara.

In 2010, Louise Prunty independently brought the first Pre-

Blended Semi Permanent Mascara to the UK. This version was called Myscara ® and did not need mixing as was already mixed in the bottle. Also this version did not need a 'dryer'. This quickly spread to many countries and manuals translated into 7 different languages.

Image from Myscara banner from China product launch.

<u>The History of Eyelash Perming</u>

Eyelash perming didn't become a widespread cosmetic treatment until after the year 2000. Exactly who created the modern perm is not known; however, many cosmetic experts state that it most likely developed in either France or Japan. The idea of lash curling, however, has been around for more than a century.

The Kurlash company are generally considered to have invented the eyelash curler; however, an earlier method was developed in 1905 by German born hairdresser Karl Nessler, who used a mixture of cow urine and water to create a product that had the chemical compounds to form curls without affecting human skin. Kessler's product wasn't, however, designed for eyelashes, though it was frequently used for lash curling purposes. It took Kessler nine years (from 1896-1905) to develop the mixture.

The first lash curler was invented sometime in the 1920s by William McDonell from Rochester, New York and his business partner Charles Stickel; however, it wasn't patented until 1931. The Kurlash company formed slightly later. Founder and chief inventor William Beldue and his business partner William R. Tuttle held several patents in Canada, the United States and

Great Britain for eyelash curlers; the first of which was filed in 1944. Over the following nine years the Kurlash company filed a further eight patents improving their product, which formed the basis of the modern eyelash curler.

Advancing Technology

In the 1970s eyelash curling technology was significantly enhanced and acid balanced perms were introduced, which were far less damaging than previous perming methods. Over the next decade many cosmetic companies jumped on the bandwagon and started developing their own variations of the Kurlash design.

Acid chemical perms were different to other methods in that they would permanently alter the structure of the eyelash. This physical change occurs when a chemical composition called keratin – a protein compromised of 19 amino acids – bonds to the lash hair amino acid crysteine. This chemical bond causes the lashes to become soft and conform to the shape of the

polypeptides, which results in a spring-like effect.

Modern Perming

Eyelash perming has been commercially available since the

early 1990s, although even today it's still not FDA approved in

some US States. Perming, however, didn't gain widespread

popularity until the 2000s. In 2001 Time Magazine published an

article discussing the demand for treatment. In 1999 the

amount of requests for eyelash perms or extensions were

merely a few per week in the average beauty parlour; however,

between then and 2001 the average amount of requests rose to

approximately 30 per day.

Administration procedures have also significantly advanced

over the last decade. In most circumstances the application of

chemicals and curling takes roughly 20 minutes; however,

many new devices have since been produced by fashion

designers to optimise the procedure; Carl Lagerfeld for instance, created his own device which provides enhanced safety and speed.

Historic Timeline of Events

10,000 BC: Ancient Egyptians started using kohl on their eyelashes to protect their eyes from sand. This birthed the first cosmetic treatments of the era, which were created using charcoal, soot, honey, water and crocodile stool.

4,000 BC: Inspired by the Egyptians, Grecian women started wearing eyelash extensions that were made from ox hair.

100-400AD: Throughout the fall of the Roman empire eyelash extensions were adorned by the rich and powerful, but considered vanity items among the lesser classes.

1800s: Cosmetic products started to grow in popularity under the reign of Queen Victoria. By the Edwardian period (1901) the illusion of darker and longer eyelashes became an obsession among upper class women.

1905: German born hairdresser Charles Nessler created the first eyelash perming chemical mixture that wasn't harmful to human skin using cow urine and water.

1911: Canadian woman Anna Taylor patented the first official eyelash extension in the United States.

1913: French chemist and perfumer Eugène Rimmel created the first non-toxic mascara. It subsequently received widespread popularity across Europe.

1915: Charles Nessler manufactured the first false eyelashes and started selling them in his New York salon.

1916: D.W. Griffith introduced eyelash extensions to the world on a global scale when he ordered his wigmaker to glue human hair to Seena Owen's lashes in the movie *Intolerance* in order to give her more of a "baby doll" look.

1917: Maybelline was born – who were to lead the eye cosmetics industry in the coming years.

1925: William McDonell and Charles Sticklel created the first lash curler.

1930: Modern mascara started to gain widespread popularity all over the world due to Helena Rubinstain, a rich woman who heavily promoted it throughout the west.

1931: William McDonell and Charles Stickel patented the first lash curler design.

1933: Maybelline started producing their first commercially available eyelash extensions, which were enjoyed by women all over the world.

Lash Lure mascara was released, which contained dangerously high levels of colouring agent paraphenylendiamine. After attempting to darken her lashes a woman named Mrs Brown was blinded.

1934: Lash Lure caused a septicaemia infection in a woman from Florida. She died in hospital three hours after it was applied.

Eyelash dyes were completely banned in the United States, resulting in the bankruptcy of several cosmetic companies.

1936: The Kurlash Co. was formed by inventor William Beldue and his business partner William R. Tuttle.

1938: The Food, Drug and Cosmetic Act was established, ensuring that advertising of cosmetic treatments were overseen by the FDA.

1944: The Kurlash Co. filed patents in the United States, Canada and Great Britain for eyelash curlers. Eight patents were filled during the following nine years.

1947: Japan's first every eyelash extensions became commercially available.

1965: Actress, model and singer Twiggy, became one of the "it girls" of Hollywood and intrigued the world with her doll-like eyelashes. Cosmetic companies started to expand their lash ranges and advertise extensions in fashion magazines.

1967: The first ever mink eyelashes were created in Japan.

1970: Acid balanced perms were invented, which were far less damaging than previous methods of perming.

1975: The first ever synthetic fibres were incorporated into false eyelashes and released in Japan.

1994: The Guild of Beauty Therapists was established in the UK and introduced new accreditations for those who had a desire to specialise in eyelash treatments.

1999: The average amount of eyelash perming requests in a typical beauty salon was less than ten per week.

1999: Mr Pashu Pang from Korea, developed and later offered training in semi permanent eyelash extensions.

2001: The average amount of eyelash perming requests in a typical beauty salon was over 30 per day.

2006: US Patent for semi permanent eyelash extensions was granted to Mr Daniel Dinh.

2007: Speedy eyelashes were invented – lashes that could be attached without any adhesive.

Eyelash extensions have had a huge impact on the cosmetics industry. While widespread popularity in the west didn't occur until the 2000s due to the general public's fascination with celebrity culture, history proves that it was being shaped and moulded for over a century. Nowadays there are literally hundreds of different brands, each with vital differences.

2009: Flexi- Glue (Flexible Glam Lash Adhesive) was introduced to the UK, developed by Caledonian Therapy Academy.

2009: 2D & 3D Lashes were invented.

Final words...

I hope you found this book useful in learning more on how eyelash extensions developed and also the history of other eye treatments.

If you have any feedback or want to keep in touch please join me on Facebook at

https://www.facebook.com/Louisepruntybiz

Please also visit www.lashinc.eu to subscribe to Lash Inc. Lash Inc is the industry eyelash journal, bringing you educational content and lash related information and images.

"It's Not Just A Skill It's An ART"

Advance Styling to Create Custom Sets of Lash Extensions

All Classes are Two Days and Offered Globally

Beginner and Advance Training

Product Knowledge | Business and Marketing Skills

Eye Anatomy | Sanitation | Eye Health

Adhesive Control | Taping Lower Lashes | Lash Layering

Full Sets vs Touch ups | Bottom Lash Application

Premium Quality Lash Products and Advance Lash Artistry Training

ArtisticLash.com
Michell@ArtisticLash.com

Premium Eyelash Extension
Products & ProfessionalTraining

The Adele Sutton Range continually strives to be the leader in the field of safe eyelash enhancements & products globally and is committed to world class Education and Products to provide safe,beautiful & flawless eyelash applications to enhance any women's natural beauty

Global Distributors:
U.S.A - Canada - U.K - Australia

Franchising Opportunities now available

www.adelesutton.com
info@adelesutton.com

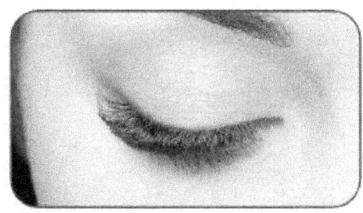 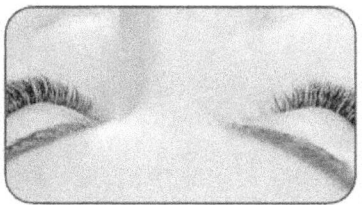 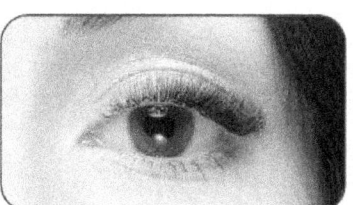